To:
Sallie + George

From:
Ruthie + Frank

Dec 25th, 1991

THE LAST CREAM BUN

A BOOK OF DRAWINGS BY ROGER PETTIWARD ('PAUL CRUM')

'Curse that fellow laughing at me; *I was just going to laugh at* him'
NIGHT AND DAY

Roger Pettiward

ROGER PETTIWARD

'PAUL CRUM'

The Last Cream Bun

A BOOK OF DRAWINGS

WITH AN INTRODUCTION BY

RUARI McLEAN

CHATTO & WINDUS

THE HOGARTH PRESS

LONDON

Published in 1984 *by*
Chatto & Windus . The Hogarth Press
40 William IV Street
London WC2N 4DF

British Library Cataloguing in Publication Data
Pettiward, Roger
The Last Cream Bun
1. English wit and humour, Pictorial
I. Title
741.5'942   NC1479

ISBN 0 7011 2907 7

*Printed in Great Britain
by W. M. Bett Ltd., Tillicoultry*

'I keep thinking it's Tuesday'
PUNCH

Introduction

ROGER PETTIWARD, born on 25 November 1906 and killed leading his commando troop at Dieppe in 1942, was an artist who signed his humorous drawings either 'Paul Crum' or with a whorl, to avoid confusion with his serious work as a painter.

For about four years, between 1935 and the beginning of the war, he contributed drawings regularly to *Punch*, *Night and Day*[1], and *London Week*[2]. A selection of these drawings are here published in book form for the first time, and show that (as the discerning realised at the time) he was a major artist. His early death was as grievous a loss to British art as the deaths in war of Eric Ravilious and Rex Whistler, and of 'Pont', whose name was linked with Pettiward by Kenneth Bird ('Fougasse', the art editor and later editor of *Punch*) who wrote 'these two, Pont and Pettiward, probably did more during this period to carry the development of modern pictorial humour a whole stage further than any two or ten or twenty others put together and it is sad that neither of them survived to see how post-war pictorial humour developed'. (Fougasse, *The Good-Tempered Pencil*, 1976).

Roger Pettiward was the second of four children, born in Suffolk into a well-to-do land-owning family. Their father was an eccentric and gifted amateur who made caricatures of local celebrities and illustrated various private journals and verses in an easy and economical style which is echoed in his son's drawings. It is related that he gave his son special tuition in the drawing of shoes and top hats. No foot, no shoe, no hat in any of Pettiward's drawings is other than beautifully drawn.

In the words of Roger's brother Daniel (kindly contributed for this essay) 'Our father, born in 1855, was a cultivated country squire of the old school; he rode round his estate daily on horseback, and would have liked his sons to grow up in his own mould, and his daughters to become ornaments of Society, but came to be proud of their achievements in other fields, mostly connected with the arts. It was a sadness to me that he died (in 1933) before Roger or I began contributing to *Punch*, which he adored.

'Our mother, twenty-five years father's junior, was a great beauty and famous for her vagueness and unpunctuality (as opposed to father's intense orderliness) . . . she was greatly loved, devoted her time to social work and amateur drama, and illustrated history books for her children when they were young . . . Cynthia, Roger's eldest sister, was an architect and teacher; Stella, a bookbinder

---

[1] *Night and Day* was an attempt to launch a London equivalent of the *New Yorker*. It was published by Chatto & Windus and while it lasted (from July to December 1937) was contributed to by leading artists and writers who rejoiced in the greater freedom available to them there than in *Punch*. It died partly because of a libel action in connection with an article by Grahame Greene about Shirley Temple.

[2] A weekly guide to events, which became *What's On*.

and actress; myself a *Punch* contributor for thirty-three years, as writer and occasional artist. Roger illustrated my first book, *Truly Rural*.' The sons, Roger and Daniel, both went to Eton and Oxford. At Eton, Roger won all the drawing prizes several times; before he left in 1925 (he was then 6' 5½" tall) he won the middle-weight boxing cup and was awarded his 'upper boat choices'. At Christ Church, Oxford, he became captain of the college boat club, and drew caricatures for the *Isis* and other university papers, and also began producing caricatures for the *Sunday Express* and the *Bystander*. He took a degree in agriculture and later a course in Farm Management at Iwerne Minster, with the intention of taking over his father's estate at Finborough in Suffolk, but finally decided on art. He studied art in Vienna (at the Academy), in Munich, at the Slade, where he married a fellow student Diana Berners-Wilson, and in Paris. At intervals he wandered off and painted in Czechoslovakia, Italy, Spain, Hungary, and Rumania; he also sailed through the Bay of Biscay down to Lisbon as one of the crew of the *Sans Pareil*, a 150-ton ketch. In addition he was an expert skier and horseman; and by 1929 had learned to fly. And he was the devoted father of a son and two daughters.

In 1932 he went as a member of an expedition to Brazil to look for Colonel Fawcett in the Matto Grosso; Peter Fleming's Foreword to *Brazilian Adventure* (the book in which he describes their adventures) ends with the words 'in particular I should like to thank Mr Roger Pettiward, who always saw the joke.' There is an excellent account, in Chapter IV, of the casual way in which Pettiward was recruited to join the expedition. After Pettiward's death, Fleming wrote in the *Spectator*: 'Very tall, with red hair and a slow quizzical drawl, Pettiward was an extraordinarily lovable and attractive person, half artist and half (in the cant term) man of action. He and I once took part in an expedition to a remote part of the world, and nothing could have exceeded the composure and resource with which he faced a series of odd and occasionally alarming predicaments. He was killed while leading "F" troop of No. 4 Commando in the successful assault on the German coastal batteries flanking Dieppe; I have been told on good authority, and I do not find it hard to believe, that if he had survived he would have been recommended for the Victoria Cross. He was a splendid person.' His second-in-command, Captain Pat Porteous, who took over command of the troop after Pettiward's death, and was wounded but survived, was awarded the V.C. The capture of the German gun positions at Varengeville was the sole success of the Dieppe raid.

In Peter Fleming's second novel *The Sixth Column*, 1951, a character occurs called 'Boy Endover', whom Fleming describes as 'a tall, rather stooping young man . . . His frivolity was so deep-rooted in him that it partook rather of the nature of a philosophy than of a failing. He appeared to believe that all human institutions, and most human situations, had in them something inherently ridiculous, and that it was his duty to exploit this latent seam of risibility . . . the mere sight of a policeman,[1] a customs official,[2] a ticket collector,[3] or a head waiter[4] automatically aroused in him an impulse of anarchy.' It seems to me

---

[1] See pages 62, 63.   [2] See page 71.

[3] See page 71.   [4] See pages 32-5.

that Fleming had Roger Pettiward at least partially in mind when he invented this character.

Pettiward found his style for humorous drawing in line, or line and wash, early, and stuck to it with very little variation. I have seen only one drawing in a different black-and-white medium, scraperboard. He did two covers in colour for *Night and Day*, and two colour pages for *Punch* Almanacs, all reproduced here; he used colour line for some commercial work, including illustrations for a booklet, *London Holiday*, published by Austin Reed and printed by Curwen Press, of which two examples are reproduced here.

Nearly all the reproductions in this book have been made direct from originals, in the possession of his family, and where possible are shown in actual size. In the case of the *Punch* drawings, it is a particular pleasure to see them in a larger size than the frustratingly minute column-width sizes to which *Punch* habitually reduced them.

The drawings have been arranged, not in chronological order, which seemed pointless since Pettiward's style did not alter significantly, but by subject. By 'subject' we mean the kind of people he put into his drawings and/or the situations into which he put them. Everyone he drew is superbly and accurately characterised both as regards face and costume, just as every chair and other property is beautifully drawn and appropriate for that occasion. From page 12 we have the 'upper classes' among whom he was brought up: note the perfection of sartorial detail — so economically drawn, yet so accurate — throughout, but perhaps especially on pages 18 and 21. From page 22 the characters tend to be in evening dress — except for the brilliantly drawn game of tennis, and the memorable old lady on page 28 — and from pages 29 to 37 they are at table. His gift for portraiture was utilised in a series of sketches for a restaurant column in *London Week* in 1935-6; some of these are shown on pages 35-7. The Cheshire Cheese, Café Royal and Prunier's are in a much more enjoyable size than that in which they appeared originally.

After meals, the washing-up (page 38); and from there until page 49 all the drawings include women, and in most of them the woman is the speaker. Again there is superb observation of detail, e.g. the glove on the lady's lap on page 42, and in the man's mouth on page 47 (which is a drawing that anyone who has ever tried to draw someone putting on a coat will particularly admire). On page 51 his focus turns to children, and on page 52 to schoolmasters in mortarboards. The three characters in 'Gosh! Are you P.K.'s mater?' (page 55), especially the boy, make this my favourite drawing in the book. On page 56 Pettiward's interest in exploration becomes the theme. The *Punch* drawing on page 59 is faced by a smaller alternative version which is in some ways funnier. On pages 60 and 61 the public schoolboys are in trouble; and from page 62 to the end of the book, what all the drawings have in common is men, in various costumes and uniforms, although there are also some remarkable women (cf. pages 69 and 71). The drawing of two firemen on page 82, with faces entirely omitted, is a good example of Pettiward's mastery in not using a line more than is needed. On page 87 is another pair of alternatives. The very scribbly large drawing is an insight into the kind of 'rough' from which his final economical drawings were evolved: it is also reminiscent of the style of Topolski, whose first drawings of

England were published in 1935 and whom Pettiward admired. It is recorded that he also admired the *Punch* artists Bert Thomas and Frank Reynolds, and the German George Grosz; and he must also have absorbed the consummate line of H. M. Bateman.

Topolski's *The London Spectacle 1935* presents a vision of London in particular, and of Britain in general, which can be usefully compared with Pettiward's vision. One wishes Pettiward had also made such a book. Topolski, just arrived from Poland, had, I think, a superficial and sentimental view of Britain; and his scenarios were suggested, albeit highly skilfully, by means almost more of notes than finished drawings. Pettiward, who knew intimately what he was drawing, and observed it accurately, stated what he wanted to say with magisterial definition: he was by far the more complete artist. For example, the village hall on page 43 (and on page 83), the consulting room on page 68, the dinner table on page 26, are all given, in exquisite detail, their most perfect characteristics. And for the results of his travels round Europe, a good example is 'our Djan' on page 81, meticulously drawn down to the trimming knife and the wood; and the Swiss ticket collector on page 71.

The artist with whom Pettiward can be more closely compared is his contemporary Nicolas Bentley. Many of Bentley's jokes (e.g. in *Die? I thought I'd laugh*, 1936, and *How can you bear to be human?*, 1957) could have been Pettiward's, and a few are virtually identical. Both artists believed that in joke drawings everything in the drawings should be funny; both were masters in this respect. Bentley can be said to have been the more comic: his drawings were often violently funny. Both were supremely successful in portraiture and costume: Bentley, in his longer career, often found his humour in witty elaborations of fancy dress and historical costume. Both could be sardonic: Bentley's more laboured line was harder and could be cruel; Pettiward's humour was the more gentle. Above all, Pettiward drew sensitively, beautifully, and easily. Pettiward was publishing drawings regularly for only four or five years: Bentley for thirty-five.

Unlike Topolski, and unlike 'Pont', Pettiward did not try consciously to portray the Britain he knew in any series; he drew people and situations that amused him, as a sideline subsidiary to his other interest, painting, which was of greater importance. But he made enough drawings, of sufficient range and humanity, to provide a genuine and moving picture of the times and places he lived in, and the people with whom he mixed.

The nineteen-thirties are evoked by these drawings: they are a distillation of the period. In Calvocoressi's and Wint's *Total War*, Penguin Books, 1972, a book written to explain the Second World War to a generation for which it was already in the fairly dim past, there occurs in Chapter 20 a significant passage which runs: 'Great Britain between the wars was not an agreeable place to live in. It was crowded with misery and injustice: estimates of the underfed in the worst years of the thirties go as high as twenty million. Little was done by government to help this large section of the nation and much of what was done was silly, for the governors were for the most part men of limited awareness and only moderate intelligence. Yet the temper of Great Britain did not become revolutionary.'

That 'Great Britain between the wars was not an agreeable place to live in' is a piece of contentious hindsight, if nothing worse; at the time many people found it intensely agreeable. Pettiward was an embodiment of the gayest and best of those times. Although a member of the privileged and governing class, he was well aware of that class's limitations, and drew with devastating accuracy many of its sillinesses; he was also, as it happens, an example of the not so common members of that governing class to whom such criticisms did not apply. His sympathies and experience of life went completely beyond the confines of class. He was a natural leader, and if Britain did not become revolutionary, it owed it to having men like him, who were of outstanding and humane calibre.

RUARI McLEAN

'Do you know of a good place to feed?'

9

'I do hope nothing happens to him.'

'There's a nasty gale in operation.'
PUNCH

'You didn't tell me we were putting on evening kit.'
NIGHT AND DAY

LONDON HOLIDAY

'Yes, Father, I know, but what virtue is there in gathering moss?'
PUNCH

'On the contrary, Lord Crabbe, I purposely didn't *call you a fool.*'
PUNCH

'I suppose they're all vaguely waterproof?'
NIGHT AND DAY

'What's the idea of having some larger than others?'
PUNCH

'*What would* you *say, Noakes, if your daughter wanted to marry a poet?*'
NIGHT AND DAY

'If only *one didn't have to wash up afterwards!*'
PUNCH

'They can't all *have forgotten;*
Cartwright Major for one wrote down the date in blood.'
PUNCH

'What's the excitement, sir — not a new Night Starvation?'
NIGHT AND DAY

'It's so difficult to look as if one was doing it for a joke without looking as if one was enjoying it.'
PUNCH

'*What's so marvellous about you is that you don't* look *like a colossal brain.*'
NIGHT AND DAY

'Thanks. I only touch marching chocolate.'
PUNCH

'I expect you knew this place when it was a snipe bog?'
PUNCH

'All right then, Lord Ronald — the next lament'
NIGHT AND DAY

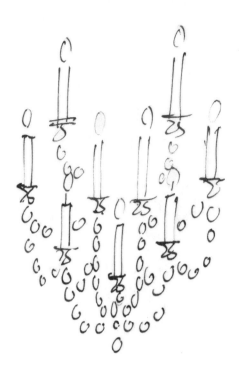

'What! No gravy?'
PUNCH

'*How do you stop these darned things showing?*'
PUNCH

'Leslie is really much the most human of the Urquharts.'
NIGHT AND DAY

'I said — I've lost my voice to-day'
LONDON WEEK

'Would it look very provincial if I were to eat my sandwiches?'
PUNCH

'*I like sucking-pig all right, but I'm afraid it doesn't like me.*'
NIGHT AND DAY

'How often must I remind you that a good wine needs no bush?'
NIGHT AND DAY

'You must pull me up if I call you shrimpson again.'
PUNCH

'Do go away — you only confuse me.'
NIGHT AND DAY

'*I thought I ordered* 青菜'
PUNCH

Paul Crum

'*Were you the stuffed neck?*'
PUNCH

'Mrs Brown, your Barsac goes to my head like wine!'
LONDON WEEK

Giacomo Prada at Casa Prada

Antoine

Oddenino's

Cheshire cheese
LONDON WEEK

Café Royal
LONDON WEEK

Prunier's
LONDON WEEK

'You certainly know how to take the "h" out of homework'
PUNCH

'You ought to be stamping out crime somewhere, not just standing there.'
PUNCH

'Someone's not concentrating'
PUNCH

'Yes, yes, but for the moment we need only discuss his replacement value.'
NIGHT AND DAY

'*Do you want me to make my mind a blank?*'
PUNCH

'Do you think there's any need to give three cheers for Miss Brown?'
NIGHT AND DAY

'Three two six George Bernard Straw — either a misprint or else a most amazing coincidence.'
PUNCH

'He used to be friendly with old Mrs Craddock when she was Fanny Parker.'
PUNCH

'. . . Take Russia.'
LONDON WEEK

'As *far as* I can make out,
Spike knew that the man with
the black moustache had done
it, but he didn't say
anything because it would have killed Spike's sister
to know that the man
with the black moustache was crooked.'
NIGHT AND DAY

'I don't suppose that group means anything to you, but it happens to be Serge Lifar on my left and Picasso behind.'
PUNCH

'I always forget whether your friend is a Pekinese or a Tangerine.'
PUNCH

49

'I'd sooner have written Gray's Elegy any day.'
NIGHT AND DAY

'I can handle Aunt Tottie; you get to work on Uncle Joe.'
NIGHT AND DAY

'If you must know, it's Joan Price.'
PUNCH

'And lastly, never dispute the umpire unless you think he's wrong.'
PUNCH

'If Johnstone's win the "footer" again, we're sunk.'
NIGHT AND DAY

'Would it interest you to see my son's report?'
'No'.
PUNCH

'Tell us something of the Great World outside Cranchester.'
PUNCH

*'I really must congratulate you, Olga's work in the loose
was nothing short of magnificent.'*
NIGHT AND DAY

'You're somewhat of a "rara avis" at Cranchester, Mrs Foster.'

54

'Gosh! Are you P.K.'s mater?'
PUNCH

'I'm afraid we close in half an hour, sir.'

'Pemmican? Yes, sir, that will be in our catering department'

56

'I warned you exploring was no picnic'
PUNCH

'Remember that time we put a mouse in his desk?'
PUNCH from different drawing

'What brought you to Patagonia, stranger?'
PUNCH

'Why must you be so darned insular?'

'*Why must you be so darned insular?*'
PUNCH

'Soake is the name; Lord Soake, I'm afraid!'
NIGHT AND DAY

*'It's pretty bleak here this term;
all the decent chaps seem to have left.'*

'You must come and meet Jock, he's just done ten years!'
NIGHT AND DAY

'All we seem to have found out so far is that his name rhymes with ompson.'
PUNCH

'There's a persistent rumour in the village that you're using a poisoned worm'
PUNCH

'It won't be long now, he's just lost another Bishop'
PUNCH

'Is that the Zoo? Well, look here — my name's Harrison.'
PUNCH

'Great Scott! Who in the world can be ringing us up?'
PUNCH

'I'm sorry — but "abracadabra" is the only magic word I know.'
NIGHT AND DAY

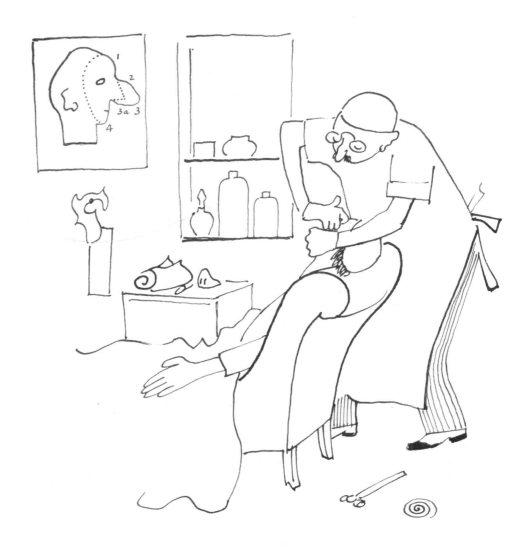

'Well, we've broken the back of it now'
NIGHT AND DAY

'Go on about your breath'
NIGHT AND DAY

'I told you not to take that last cream bun, and now, needless to say, you're beginning to regret it.'
NIGHT AND DAY

'I'm afraid one of you would have to stand down,
we couldn't do with more than one Foreign Secretary.'
PUNCH

Paul Crum

'He's only tolerated on account of his rice-puddings'
PUNCH

'Will you drop us off at Aunt Barbara's Tea Kitchen?'
PUNCH

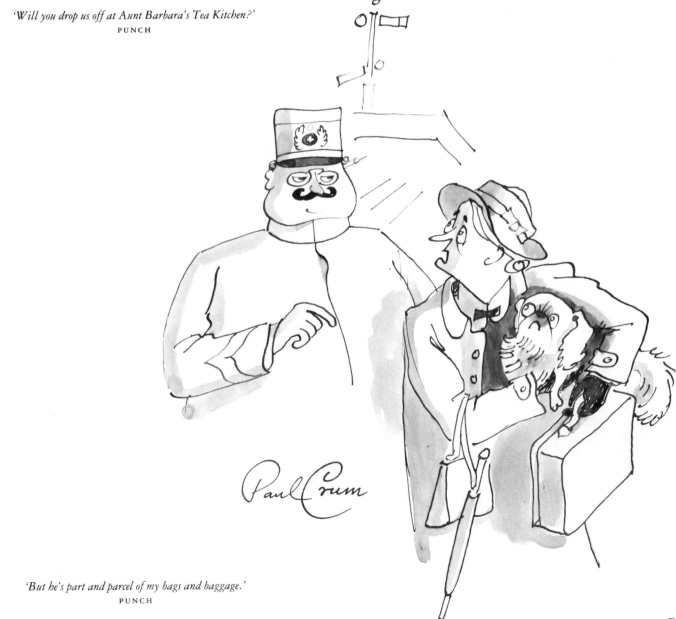

'But he's part and parcel of my bags and baggage.'
PUNCH

'D'you want me to be perfectly frank, Bishop?'
NIGHT AND DAY

'We're going to look pretty silly if it's the wrong day'
PUNCH

'As soon as it gets out that we're refacing the apse some hothead will want us to do the chancel'
PUNCH

'Mr and Mrs Crum regret that they cannot attend the festival
as it is not quite their cup of tea.'
PUNCH

'Did I or did I not say "Non Troppo"?'
PUNCH

'Don't take it so hard, new fellows always get ragged a bit at first'
PUNCH

LONDON WEEK

'Who was that foreign-looking fellow who insisted
on seeing the plans?'
PUNCH

'Ah, you want Smith, J. Gngrcr; this is Smith J. Chntmkr'
PUNCH

'I feel there must be a solution'
PUNCH

'For God's sake stop calling me little woman'
NIGHT AND DAY, different drawing

'One gets awfully fit doing this'
NIGHT AND DAY

NIGHT AND DAY

'A balaclava is always safe, sir'
NIGHT AND DAY

'I can't help feeling proud of our Djan,
even though he is a Dictator'
NIGHT AND DAY

LONDON WEEK

'Something to do with the gas, isn't it?'
NIGHT AND DAY

"WE'LL GET THE HUN, HUN, HUN ON THE RUN"

"WE'LL CLIMB UP THE STAIRS WITH OUR DOLLIES AND BEARS"

'I don't know what to do with Catchpole, Sir; he just keeps smiling through.'

'I shall monkey around with the face for another couple of days and if it still looks like a boot I *shall* most likely scrap the whole thing.'
NIGHT AND DAY

85

'You swan-herds are all the same.'
NIGHT AND DAY

'Oughtn't I to say Yoicks or something?'

'This is hardly the time for jokes of that sort'
NIGHT AND DAY

LONDON HOLIDAY

'Then, seeing that things were going against us, I sounded my horn'
(unpublished)

'Next take a stout saw'

PUNCH

Rough sketch, possibly for a NIGHT AND DAY cover

The Eton and Harrow cricket match
NIGHT AND DAY cover design

Some northern animals in their summer and winter dress
(with apologies to the Natural History Museum)
PUNCH

94

Grouse shoot
NIGHT AND DAY cover

Rough sketch (unpublished) for LONDON HOLIDAY